What in the WOW?! 2:

250 **MORE** Bonkerballs Facts

**By Mindy Thomas and Guy Raz
with Thomas van Kalken
Illustrated by Dave Coleman**

Clarion Books
An Imprint of HarperCollinsPublishers

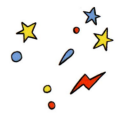

CONTENTS

Introduction	1
1. Animals	3
2. Space	21
3. Dinosaurs	33
4. Food! Ah!!	37
5. Nature	45
6. Big Mistakes	53
7. Collections and Oddities	59
8. Human Ancestry	73
9. Medicine	83
10. Poop	99
11. Presidents	109
12. History	121
13. Mysteries	133
14. Beaches	141
15. Geography	153
16. Language	167
17. Weird Laws	179
18. Roller Coasters	189
19. Just Bonkerballs	195

INTRODUCTION
Welcome to another edition of What in the WOW?!

PSST! Hey you! Yeah, you!

Thank you for cracking open this book and giving us some fresh air!

Yeah, it was getting a little stuffy in here. Hi! I'm Mindy Thomas!

And I'm Guy Raz. And together, we make a podcast called Wow in the World!

We also made you this bonkerballs book!

Now, before you dive in, there are a few things you should know.

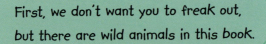

ANIMALS

Female bats give birth **UPSIDE DOWN**, catching their baby bats in their wings as they drop!

The **Wood Frog** can HOLD ITS PEE for up to eight months.

Pigs don't **SWEAT**.

Sharks have been AROUND LONGER THAN TREES.

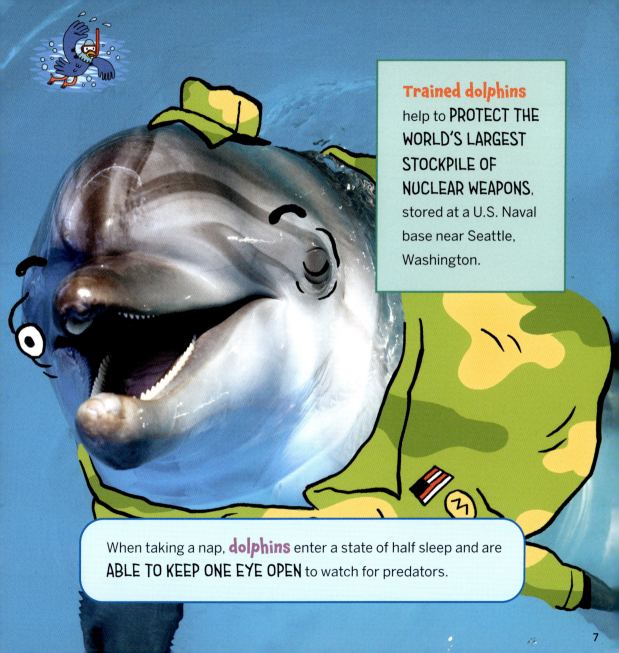

Trained dolphins help to PROTECT THE WORLD'S LARGEST STOCKPILE OF NUCLEAR WEAPONS, stored at a U.S. Naval base near Seattle, Washington.

When taking a nap, **dolphins** enter a state of half sleep and are ABLE TO KEEP ONE EYE OPEN to watch for predators.

For nearly 20 years, a **ginger cat** named Stubbs was MAYOR OF THE ALASKAN TOWN OF TALKEETNA.

According to a Japanese study, looking at **pictures of cute animals** can help BOOST YOUR ABILITY TO FOCUS.

A **group of ferrets** is called a "BUSINESS."

A **blue whale's heart** weighs about **400 POUNDS**— as heavy as a full-grown male lion! And that's just **1 PERCENT OF ITS BODY WEIGHT,** which is 40,000 pounds!

Disneyland in California was once **HOME TO OVER 200 FERAL CATS,** which helped control the rodent population—watch out Mickey! Now, the wild cat population is less than 100.

There was a species of **ancient penguins** that STOOD MORE THAN FIVE FEET TALL, about as big as adult humans!

"THAT SHOULD HELP STOP THE BLEEDING."

Ancient Greeks and **Romans** used SPIDERWEBS AS BANDAGES to treat cuts.

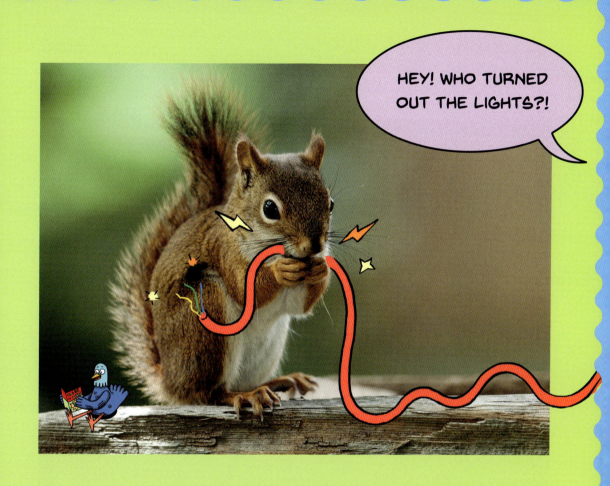

Squirrels are among the TOP CAUSES OF POWER OUTAGES in the U.S.

The **warty comb jellyfish** has a DISAPPEARING BUTT.
Its butt only appears when it needs to poop!

Cows KILL MORE PEOPLE every year than sharks do.

When swallowed by toads, **bombardier beetles** SPEW HOT, TOXIC CHEMICALS FROM THEIR BUTTS, which sometimes forces the predators to barf them back up.

Technically, **King Charles III** owns all the DOLPHINS AND SWANS IN THE UNITED KINGDOM!

"Frito Feet" is a term used to describe the phenomenon of dog feet that SMELL LIKE CORN CHIPS.

Can I get some guacamole for these dog feet?

SPACE

Astronauts drink their **OWN PEE!** The urine of all the astronauts and laboratory animals on the International Space Station is **FILTERED BACK INTO THE DRINKING-WATER SUPPLY.**

Saturn could technically **FLOAT IN A BATHTUB OF WATER,** but it is impossible to build a bathtub big enough to hold Saturn.

Buzz Aldrin was the FIRST PERSON TO PEE THEIR PANTS on the moon.

Astronauts on the International Space Station **DON'T HAVE TO SIT TO EAT** because it's easier to stay afloat in microgravity.

If they prefer an Earth-like dining experience, they need thigh and foot straps to stay seated and use magnetic or Velcro trays and utensils to eat.

Dust storms on Mars are the LARGEST IN THE ENTIRE SOLAR SYSTEM and can last for months.

Astronauts wear DIAPERS DURING LAUNCH AND SPACEWALKS.

Neptune, the windiest planet, has **GIANT, SPINNING STORMS** that are technically large enough to swallow the Earth whole!

Uranus smells like **ROTTEN EGGS**.

"Who tooted?"

"Ugh! Smells like rotten eggs!"

BRAAAP!

IT'S HYDROGEN SULFIDE!

Astronauts aboard the Apollo missions had PLASTIC BAGS TAPED TO THEIR BUTTS to capture their poop.

Sometimes it "snows" carbon dioxide on MARS.

Apollo 17 astronaut **Harrison Schmitt** was ALLERGIC TO MOON DUST.

The **microgravity of space** can cause your BLOOD TO FLOW BACKWARD.

In space, **your farts** can be FLAMMABLE.

DINOSAURS

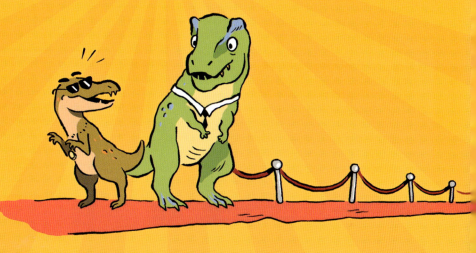

Dinosaurs could GROW NEW TEETH EVERY COUPLE OF MONTHS to replace any that were broken or damaged.

WE DON'T EVEN NEED A DENTIST.

WHAT'S A DENTIST?

In the movie *Jurassic Park*, **dinosaurs** are only on SCREEN FOR 15 MINUTES.

JURASSIC PARK TONIGHT!

IT'S OUR 15 MINUTES OF FAME!

Mary Anning (1799–1847) was ONE OF THE MOST FAMOUS FOSSIL HUNTERS OF ALL TIME. But she was never taken seriously because she was a woman from a poor background, whereas most scientists were men from wealthy families.

BABY BRAINED!

A **newborn human baby** has a **BIGGER BRAIN** than most adult dinosaurs.

It's so cute I'm gonna barf!

Almost all dinosaurs made NESTS TO SLEEP IN AND LAID EGGS.

FOOD! AH!!

Roasted ants replace popcorn as a **POPULAR MOVIE SNACK** in the South American country of Colombia.

Eggplants are BERRIES.

Bacon was used to make EXPLOSIVES DURING WORLD WAR II.

The **world's heaviest lemon** weighed ALMOST 12 LBS (5.4 kg). That's more than the average house cat!

In Italy, it is considered **bad luck** to lay A LOAF OF BREAD UPSIDE DOWN.

Several **ancient bakers** used TO STAMP THEIR BREAD IN ORDER TO COMBAT "BREAD FRAUD" and so the bread could be traced in case it turned out to be infected or moldy.

The **tiny seeds** on strawberries are NOT ACTUALLY SEEDS—they're fruits!

This is just a bowl of seeds!

Actually, it's the world's smallest fruit salad.

Bubblegum is pink because it was the ONLY COLOR OF DYE AVAILABLE IN THE FACTORY where it was invented!

In 1953, it took a whopping **27 HOURS** to produce **one Peeps chick**. Today this process takes only six minutes.

The **Ms** in M&Ms STAND FOR "MARS & MURRIE."

Americans eat an average of **100 ACRES OF PIZZA EVERY DAY.**

NATURE

About 71 percent of the world is made of **water**, but LESS THAN 1 PERCENT IS SAFE FOR HUMAN CONSUMPTION.

It takes about **TWO AND A HALF YEARS** to grow just **one pineapple**!

Be patient, Mindy!

Come on! I need you for my pizza!

They may look light and fluffy, but according to some researchers a **single cloud** could **WEIGH MORE THAN A MILLION POUNDS.**

Hey, Guy Raz! A little help, please?!

Bristlecone pine trees can live for
MORE THAN 5,000 YEARS.

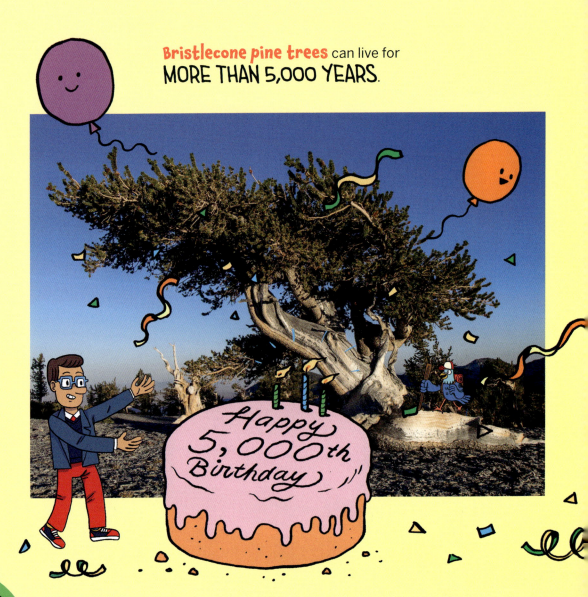

According to a 2015 study, a **city block with ten or more trees** can make a PERSON LIVING THERE FEEL SEVEN YEARS YOUNGER.

The **smell of fresh-cut grass** is due to the CHEMICALS IT RELEASES WHILE UNDER DISTRESS.

At the **Poison Garden** in England, some of the plants are so deadly, THEY'RE GROWN IN CAGES.

A **moonbow** is a RAINBOW THAT OCCURS AT NIGHT.

Some say that there's a Crock-pot of silver at the end of it!

BIG MISTAKES

BOBBY LEACH.
SECOND PERSON TO RIDE DOWN
NIAGARA FALLS IN A BARREL.
DEATH BY ORANGE PEEL.

In September 1999, after 10 months of traveling, **NASA's Mars Climate Orbiter** BURNED UP UPON ORBITAL ENTRY TO THE RED PLANET. Why? Because the engineers that designed the $125 million vessel used **IMPERIAL MEASUREMENTS**... and NASA scientists used **METRIC UNITS!**

Bobby Leach, the second person to go DOWN NIAGARA FALLS IN A BARREL AND LIVE, later died by slipping on an ORANGE PEEL.

BOBBY LEACH. SECOND PERSON TO RIDE DOWN NIAGARA FALLS IN A BARREL. DEATH BY ORANGE PEEL.

In 1895, there were **only two cars** on the road in the entire state of Ohio, and the DRIVERS OF THOSE TWO CARS CRASHED THEIR VEHICLES INTO EACH OTHER.

NASA ACCIDENTALLY TAPED OVER the **original recordings** of the moon landing.

In the 1904 Summer Olympics, marathoner **Fred Lorz** won the gold medal (at least for a little while) despite having **TAKEN A TAXI FROM MILE 9 TO MILE 18**.

COLLECTIONS AND ODDITIES

The **largest padlock** in the world WEIGHS 916 POUNDS.

A **cornflake** in the shape of Illinois SOLD ON eBAY FOR $1,350.

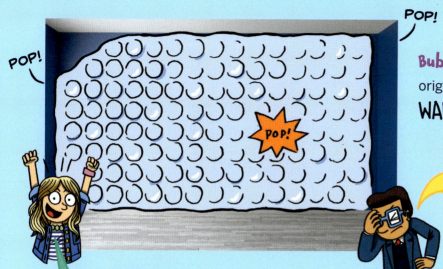

Bubble wrap was originally invented as WALLPAPER.

One of the **earliest vacuum cleaners** was so large and heavy that it was PULLED VIA A HORSE-DRAWN CARRIAGE.

The **Goodyear Blimp** is the OFFICIAL BIRD of Redondo Beach, California.

At least **one color** of the **Olympic rings** appears on EVERY COUNTRY'S FLAG. Can you find yours?

McDonald's first introduced **drive-through service** due to the military. Soldiers **WEREN'T ALLOWED TO WEAR THEIR FATIGUES IN PUBLIC** and it seemed like a waste of time to change into civilian clothes. So, a franchise near a military base in Sierra Vista, Arizona, started offering food via drive-through.

There is a **concrete bridge** in Germany that is **PAINTED TO LOOK LIKE GIANT LEGO BRICKS,** and you can totally walk and drive across it.

The **U.S. National Tick Collection**, located in Statesboro, Georgia, is HOME TO THE WORLD'S LARGEST COLLECTION OF TICKS—over one million individual specimens from all over the globe!

A **fortune cookie company** once FORETOLD THE LOTTERY, resulting in 110 winners.

In Japan, there is a belief that if a **sumo wrestler** can MAKE YOUR BABY CRY, it means he or she will live a healthy life.

A **parakeet diaper**, a **baby-patting machine**, and an **alarm clock that squirts the sleeper's face** are ALL INVENTIONS THAT HAVE BEEN GRANTED PATENTS in the United States.

The **Mustard Museum** in Middleton, Wisconsin, houses a COLLECTION OF OVER 5,624 VARIETIES OF MUSTARD.

See-through playing cards, **sleeping bags for bats**, and **rounded scissors for faster haircuts** are among the INTENTIONALLY USELESS INVENTIONS that can be found at the Nonseum in Herrnbaumgarten, Austria.

If you travel to Malmö, Sweden, during the holidays, you might be **GREETED BY A 20-FOOT-TALL** (6 m) *talking lamp* that resides in the town's square to welcome Christmas.

The **Coromoto Ice Cream Shop** in Merida, Venezuela, is home to the **WORLD'S LARGEST NUMBER OF ICE CREAM FLAVORS,** including smoked trout, hot dog, and fried pork rind!

In the early 90s, **Pepsi** **MADE A DEAL WITH THE SOVIET UNION:** 17 submarines, a cruiser, and two warships all for a little soda pop!

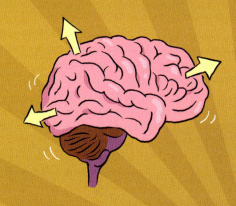

HUMAN ANCESTRY

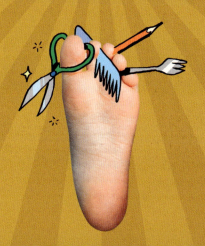

You might just be PART NEANDERTHAL!

About 50,000 years ago, **humans** first set out upon the high seas, traveling from what is today **SOUTHEAST ASIA TO AUSTRALIA**.

About 80,000 years ago, there was a **big cataclysmic event** that **NEARLY WIPED OUT THE HUMAN RACE**. Scientists still aren't sure what this was.

Humans are STILL EVOLVING! In fact, some scientists believe that we may currently be evolving faster than ever before.

Human baby hair contains TRACES OF GOLD.

Only **2 PERCENT OF THE HUMAN POPULATION** has **green eyes**, and they're most common in females.

Humans have only ever **ELIMINATED ONE DISEASE: SMALLPOX.**

WE DID IT!

NO SMALLPOX!

About **7 percent of all humans** who have ever existed ARE ALIVE RIGHT NOW.

Humans have been **HUNTER-GATHERERS** for 99 percent of their entire existence.

It took **humans 100,000 years** to reach a POPULATION OF 1 BILLION PEOPLE. By comparison, it took just 12 years for the world's population to grow from 6 billion to 7 billion.

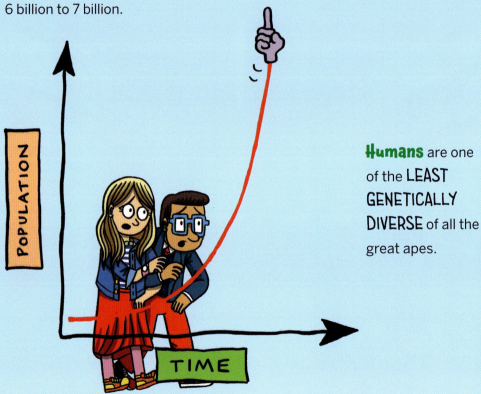

Humans are one of the LEAST GENETICALLY DIVERSE of all the great apes.

Today, the **population of New York City** is MORE THAN THE POPULATION of the ENTIRE WORLD 10,000 years ago.

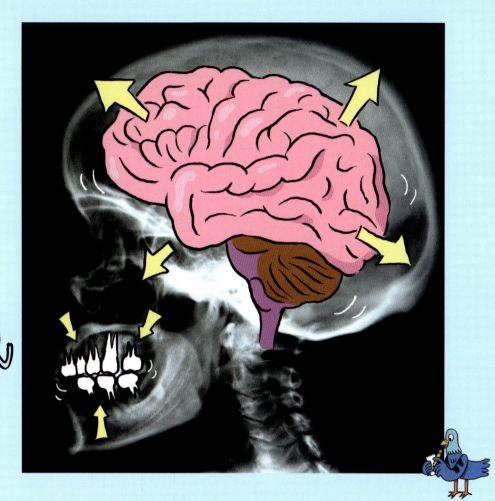

As humans have evolved, **our tooth size** has GOTTEN SMALLER whereas **our brains** have GOTTEN LARGER.

Human beings have been AROUND FOR ABOUT 300,000 YEARS. By comparison, the **Neanderthal** was around for MORE THAN 400,000 YEARS before going extinct.

And that's nothing compared to **Homo erectus**, who was AROUND FOR ABOUT 1.5 MILLION YEARS before going extinct.

About **8 percent of the population** might have a MUSCLE IN THEIR FOOT that would have allowed their ape ancestors to grip things with their toes.

MEDICINE

The average **red blood cell** lives for about **120 DAYS**.

blah blah blah

When you **speak to yourself in your head**, or in your inner voice, the MUSCLES IN YOUR LARYNX (VOICE BOX) MOVE A LITTLE.

Every square inch of the **human body** is COVERED IN ABOUT 1 BILLION BACTERIA.

We're crawling with it.

Signals from **your brain** travel at more than 250 MPH (400 KPH).

Identical twins have IDENTICAL DNA but NOT IDENTICAL FINGERTIPS.

If **you farted** consistently for 6 years and 9 months, you would have created **ENOUGH GAS TO EQUAL THE ENERGY OF AN ATOMIC BOMB.**

ALMOST THERE!

TOOT!

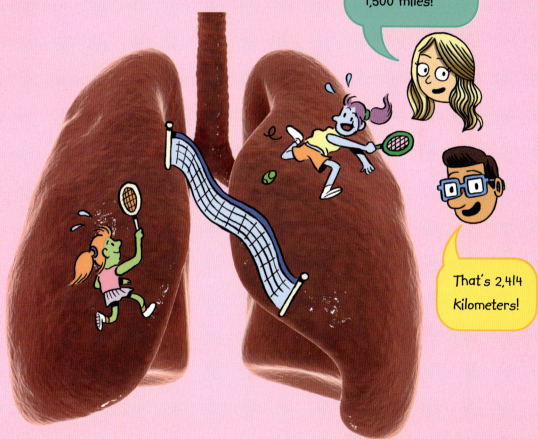

Red blood cells can TRAVEL THROUGH YOUR ENTIRE BODY in under 20 seconds.

At least 2 million new **red blood cells** are CREATED IN YOUR BODY EVERY SECOND. That's the population of Houston, Texas!

When you **blush**, your STOMACH LINING ALSO REDDENS.

Out of all the nails on your body, the **thumbnail GROWS THE SLOWEST** and the **middle fingernail GROWS THE FASTEST.**

One quarter of all your **bones** are LOCATED IN YOUR FEET!

The **force of gravity** makes your EARS AND NOSE GROW LONGER for your whole lifetime!

In a lifetime, **human beings** will GROW 6 FEET OF NOSE HAIR.

A cry is **good for you**!

Crying actually SHEDS STRESS HORMONES.

The **average life span** for a strand of hair is **2 TO 7 YEARS**.

Women blink nearly TWICE AS MUCH AS MEN.

MORE MEN THAN WOMEN are **left-handed**.

BIGGEST BLINKER

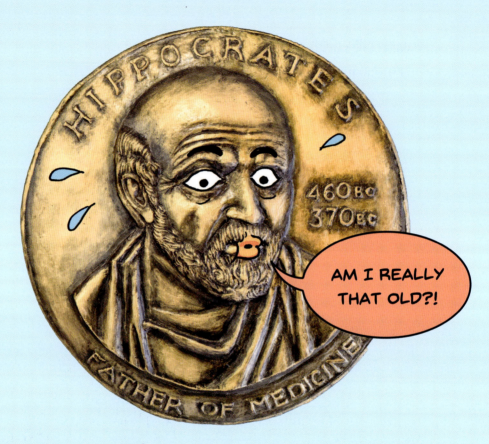

The **Hippocratic Oath**, which is a promise that medical students take to help people when they become doctors, was ORIGINALLY WRITTEN OVER 2,000 YEARS AGO.

We **LOSE 30,000 TO 40,000 dead skin cells** every minute. That means we lose around 50 million cells every day!

The **human heart** BEATS AROUND 100,000 TIMES A DAY or 35 million times a year.

The **average person farts** enough TO FILL ONE BIRTHDAY PARTY BALLOON EACH DAY. That's about 23 ounces (700 ml) of gas!

POOP

Up to 80 percent of your **poop** is BACTERIA and not just old food.

I always thought it was because of all the chocolate I ate.

Poop is brown because that's the COLOR OF DEAD RED BLOOD CELLS.

The outside of **corn kernels** is COVERED IN A MATERIAL CALLED CELLULOSE. This coating protects them from various stomach acids and is why you can sometimes see them in your poop.

The **ideal poop**, according to science, is a CONTINUOUS LOG THAT SINKS TO THE BOTTOM OF THE TOILET BOWL.

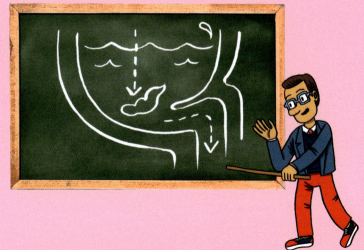

Pandas poop as much as **40 TIMES** a day.

In 2006, **President George W. Bush** reportedly had his own **PERSONAL TOILET SHIPPED TO AUSTRIA,** for his state visit, out of a fear that people would try to capture and examine his poop.

28,000 pounds of poop is SCHLEPPED OFF MOUNT EVEREST every single year.

Humans can poop anywhere from **THREE TIMES A DAY TO THREE TIMES A WEEK**. Neither more frequent nor less frequent pooping is healthier than the other.

The **average person** will poop around **25,000 POUNDS** in their lifetime.

Sloths only POOP ONCE A WEEK, and they DO A LITTLE DANCE as they do it.

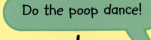

Do the poop dance!

Coffee beans that have been INGESTED AND THEN POOPED OUT by the Asian Palm civet cat can cost up to $600 a pound or $100 for a single cup.

HEE HEE

PRESIDENTS

Richard Nixon was a great musician and **PLAYED FIVE DIFFERENT INSTRUMENTS:** piano, saxophone, clarinet, accordion, and violin.

President Abraham Lincoln was a **SKILLED WRESTLER** and honored with an award from the National Wrestling Hall of Fame in 1992—which was 127 years after he died.

Abraham Lincoln turned down an opportunity to **POPULATE THE UNITED STATES WITH ELEPHANTS.**

THE FIRST PRESIDENT WAS NOT THE FIRST FACE TO APPEAR ON THE $1 BILL! That honor belongs to **Salmon P. Chase**, who was Secretary of Treasury in 1862 when the bill was introduced.

President Ronald Reagan was a strong BELIEVER IN ASTROLOGY.

Presidents John Adams and **Thomas Jefferson** both PASSED AWAY ON JULY 4, 1826.

President Zachary Taylor passed away after eating far **TOO MANY CHERRIES AND DRINKING MILK** at a Fourth of July party in 1850.

President Calvin Coolidge had many pets, including **TWO LIONS!** Their names were Tax Reduction and Budget Bureau.

President Theodore Roosevelt's daughter Alice had a **PET SNAKE NAMED EMILY SPINACH.** She would keep Emily Spinach in her purse, carrying him around the White House and using him to surprise unsuspecting guests.

President Ronald Reagan's favorite candy was JELLY BELLY JELLYBEANS. In fact, **3.5 TONS OF RED, WHITE, AND BLUE CANDIES WERE SHIPPED TO WASHINGTON, D.C.,** for his inauguration in 1981. During his presidency, **720 BAGS OF JELLYBEANS** were delivered to the White House and distributed to government buildings around Capitol Hill.

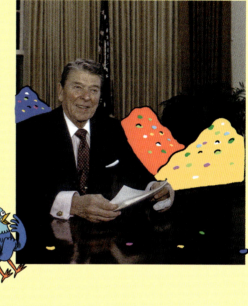

Ronald Reagan's FIRST JOB WAS AS A LIFEGUARD. Over those six years, he saved **77 PEOPLE** from drowning.

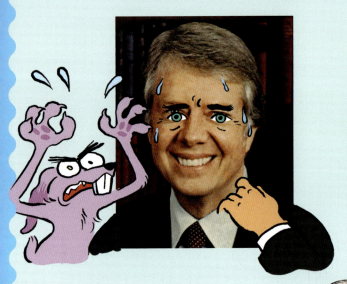

President Jimmy Carter was ATTACKED BY A GIANT SWIMMING RABBIT in 1979 while fishing in his hometown of Plains, Georgia.

George Washington's famous dentures were actually made of GOLD, IVORY, LEAD, HORSE TEETH, HIPPO BONE, AND DONKEY TEETH— not wood!

HIPPO BONE

HISTORY

The **verb "unfriend"** dates all the way BACK TO 1659.

In 300 BC, **Mayans** used to WORSHIP TURKEYS as if they were gods.

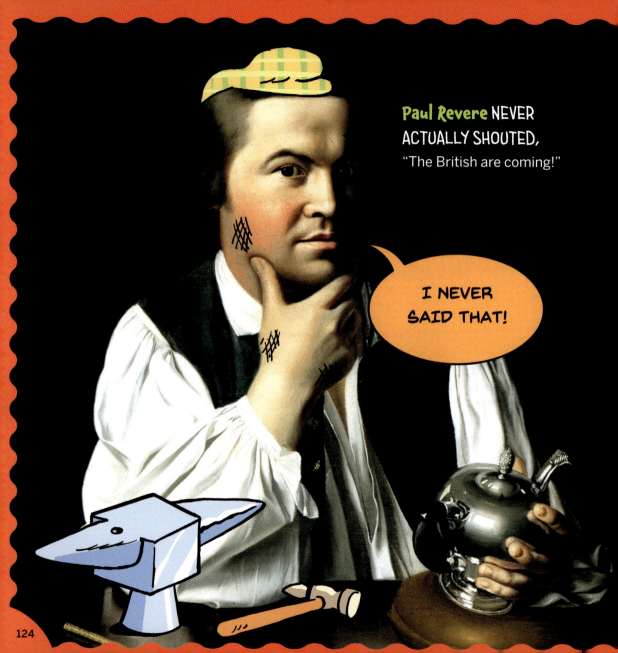

From 1912 to 1948, the **Olympic Games** held COMPETITIONS IN THE FINE ARTS. Medals were given for literature, architecture, sculpture, painting, and music.

Napoleon Bonaparte was **ATTACKED BY . . . BUNNIES.** In a rabbit hunt gone wrong, hundreds of captured bunny rabbits, when released, **CHARGED AT NAPOLEON AND HIS MEN,** injuring several soldiers.

Cleopatra was **NOT EGYPTIAN;** she was actually Greek.

Cleopatra wore **LIPSTICK MADE WITH CRUSHED-UP ANTS AND BEETLES.**

In the early 13th century, **Pope Gregory IX** DECLARED A WAR ON CATS because he believed they were satanic and associated with witchcraft.

A woman named **Jeannette Rankin** was ELECTED TO THE U.S. CONGRESS BEFORE WOMEN COULD EVEN VOTE.

In the early 19th century, people among the upper class would sometimes **DECORATE THEIR HOMES AND BUSINESSES** with *Egyptian mummies*.

MYSTERIES

The **Great Sphinx of Giza** is AMONG THE LARGEST STATUES TO SURVIVE FROM THE ANCIENT WORLD. It was covered by sand for thousands of years, until the first modern attempt to dig it out in 1817. Imagine what else is lying under our feet!

In July 1518, people in Strasbourg were infected with the **Dancing Plague**. Leaders in the community believed that **MORE DANCING COULD HELP BREAK THEIR FEVERS;** they even created dance halls and hired bands to accompany the sick dancers. But that only made it worse. As many as **400 PEOPLE** danced themselves to death!

Amelia Earhart was the **FIRST WOMAN TO FLY ACROSS THE ATLANTIC OCEAN**. But in July 1937, **SHE DISAPPEARED** somewhere over the Pacific Ocean, never to be seen again.

On November 7, 1872, **Captain Benjamin Briggs**, **his wife**, **their 2-year-old daughter**, and ten others set sail from New York City to Genoa, Italy, and **WERE NEVER SEEN AGAIN**. Stranger still, a month later their **SHIP WAS FOUND FLOATING IN THE MIDDLE OF THE OCEAN** with not a soul on board.

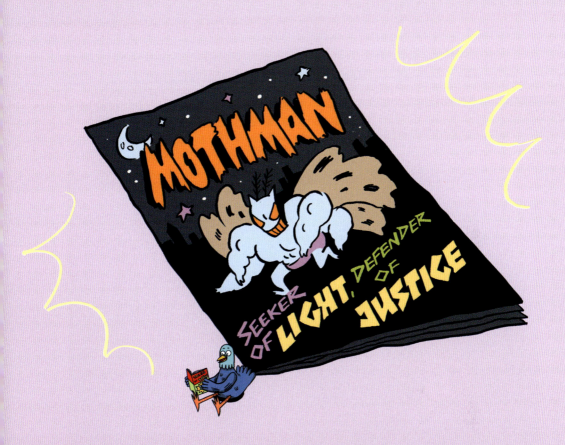

Between November 15, 1966, and December 15, 1967, numerous sightings of a **HUGE, BIRD-LIKE CREATURE WITH GLOWING RED EYES** were reported near Point Pleasant, West Virginia. The creature was dubbed the **Mothman**.

John White and more than 100 colonists **ARRIVED AT ROANOKE ISLAND,** North Carolina, in 1587. Later that year John headed back to England to get more supplies. **WHEN HE RETURNED IN 1590, NO ONE WAS HOME!** The entire village had been abandoned.

BEACHES

A company called **Skulptura Projects** made the TALLEST SANDCASTLE IN THE WORLD on June 5, 2019, in Binz, Germany. It measured **57 FEET AND 11 INCHES (17.65 M)** TALL.

Shell Beach in Australia is made up of BILLIONS OF TINY SHELLS.

In the Maldives, there is a **beach** that literally GLOWS IN THE DARK!

Thanks to **lifeguards**, more than 100,000 PEOPLE ARE SAVED from drowning each year in the U.S. alone!

There are **four beaches** in the world with GREEN SAND.

More than **400 MILLION PEOPLE** visit **beaches** in the U.S. each year.

Beaches may be on the way out! Some scientists think that because of **RISING SEA LEVELS** and **OTHER CLIMATE CHANGE EVENTS,** half of the world's beaches will be **NON-EXISTENT** by the end of the century.

Facing a surge in *unprovoked shark attacks*, Australia is now **DEPLOYING SHARK-DETECTING DRONES** above its most popular beaches.

In 2008, an **entire beach** was **STOLEN** in Jamaica. Over 500 truckloads of sand were taken from the shore!

There is an uninhabited Caribbean Island in the Bahamas known as **Pig Beach**, which is POPULATED ENTIRELY BY SWIMMING PIGS!

GEOGRAPHY

In Wisconsin, **Ho-Chunk** and other **First Nations people** have MINED FOR LEAD IN THE SOUTHWEST REGION OF THE STATE for hundreds to thousands of years.

When **colonizers** arrived in the state, some LEAD MINERS WOULD SPEND THEIR WINTERS IN MINING TUNNELS DUG INTO HILLS, earning them the NICKNAME "BADGERS," just like the animal that would also burrow into hillsides. That's why it's nicknamed the "Badger State"!

The term **"Gruen Transfer"** describes the **FEELING OF LOSING TRACK OF TIME AND PLACE.** Shopping malls are designed with this in mind.

The **heads on Easter Island** all have BODIES.

Boring, Oregon; **Dull**, Scotland; and **Bland Shire**, Australia, are all MEMBERS OF THE LEAGUE OF EXTRAORDINARY COMMUNITIES.

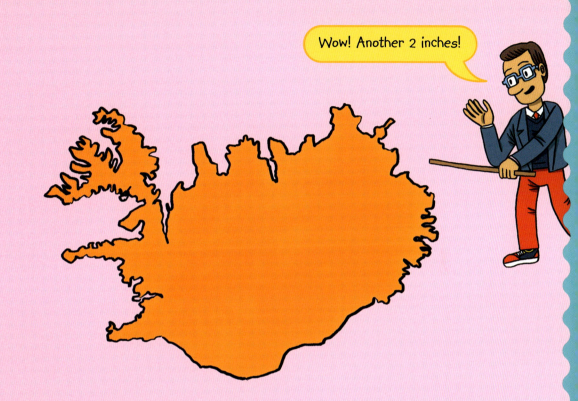

There are three towns in the world that are **JUST ONE LETTER LONG!** The town of Å, which means "river," in Norway; the town of Ö, which means "island," in Sweden; and the French village of Y.

Only **two countries** in South America DON'T BORDER BRAZIL.

The **Australian Alps** get MORE SNOW THAN THE SWISS ALPS.

The **sacred Paga Crocodile Pond** of Paga, Ghana, is home to the world's only known DOCILE CROCODILES.

Igloo City is a never-finished, empty, and ABANDONED HOTEL LOCATED IN REMOTE ALASKA.

LANGUAGE

SLEEPING THROUGH THE SUMMER is called **estivation**.

Say cheese — not so fast!

In the Victorian era, people would say "PRUNES!" BEFORE HAVING THEIR PICTURE TAKEN.

Floccinaucinihilipilification is a word used to describe **SOMETHING THAT'S WORTHLESS.** It's also one of the **LONGEST WORDS** in the English language.

Four is the only number with the SAME AMOUNT OF LETTERS AS THE MEANING of its name.

A **"lawn mullet"** is used to describe A YARD THAT IS FRESHLY CUT IN THE FRONT, but an OVERGROWN MESS IN THE BACK.

The word **"dude"** originated in the 1800s as a term used to describe MEN WHO WERE OBSESSED WITH THE LATEST FASHION TRENDS.

In Scotland, the word **"tartle"** is used to describe **THE PANIC SENSATION OF FORGETTING SOMEONE'S NAME** when you see them.

HELLO MY NAME IS

TARTLE

The Spangler Candy Company named their lollipops **"Dum Dums"** because it was **EASY FOR KIDS TO SAY.**

173

The **Busuu language** of the African nation of Cameroon is only SPOKEN BY EIGHT PEOPLE, according to a 2005 survey.

There is NO OFFICIAL LANGUAGE OF THE UNITED STATES, though **English** is the most widely spoken language. In comparison, **Bolivia** has the MOST OFFICIAL LANGUAGES, WITH 37!

Rotokas is the language with the shortest alphabet. It only has **12 LETTERS** and it's **SPOKEN IN PAPUA NEW GUINEA.** In comparison, **Khmer** has the longest alphabet with **74 LETTERS!** It is **SPOKEN IN CAMBODIA.**

The word **"alphabet"** is derived from the GREEK LETTERS "ALPHA" AND "BETA," which are the first two letters in their alphabet.

More English speakers live in **NIGERIA** than in the **U.K.**

Silbo Gomero is a language used by the people of La Gomera in the Canary Islands. This language DOESN'T USE ANY WORDS; instead, people COMMUNICATE THROUGH WHISTLES!

According to the Oxford English Dictionary, **"publicly"** is the **MOST COMMONLY MISSPELLED** word in the English language.

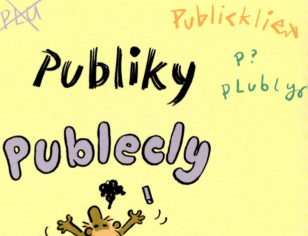

Back in the 15th century, **magicians** were CALLED "JUGGLERS."

WEIRD LAWS

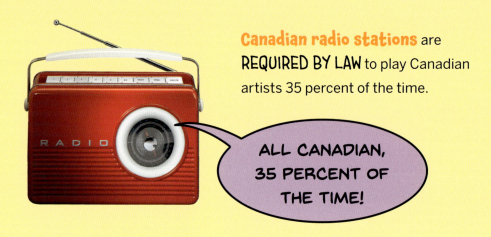

Canadian radio stations are **REQUIRED BY LAW** to play Canadian artists 35 percent of the time.

ALL CANADIAN, 35 PERCENT OF THE TIME!

Christmas was once **OUTLAWED IN MASSACHUSETTS,** as it was considered an ancient pagan holiday.

It is **ILLEGAL TO WEAR A SUIT OF ARMOR** into **Parliament** in England.

It is required by law that you **WALK YOUR DOG ONCE A DAY** in Rome. If an owner does not walk their dog once a day (at minimum), they could be fined $625.

In Turin, an Italian city farther north, you must walk your dog **THREE TIMES** a day!

Although no one has ever captured proof that Bigfoot exists, it is **ILLEGAL TO KILL BIGFOOT** in BC, Canada.

It is **ILLEGAL TO PEE** in the ocean in **Portugal**.

Unless you have a permit, it is **ILLEGAL TO CLIMB TREES** in **Toronto, Canada**.

That reminds me of a joke!

It is **ILLEGAL FOR A CHICKEN TO CROSS THE ROAD** in **Quitman, Georgia**. Or rather, if your chickens get loose, you could receive a hefty fine.

Oh boy . . .

In **Canada**, it is **ILLEGAL TO MAKE A PAYMENT OF MORE THAN $10** with more than a single coin.

In **Switzerland**, it's ILLEGAL TO OWN ONLY ONE GUINEA PIG because they get lonely.

In the state of **California**, it is ILLEGAL TO EAT A FROG THAT DIES DURING A FROG-JUMPING CONTEST.

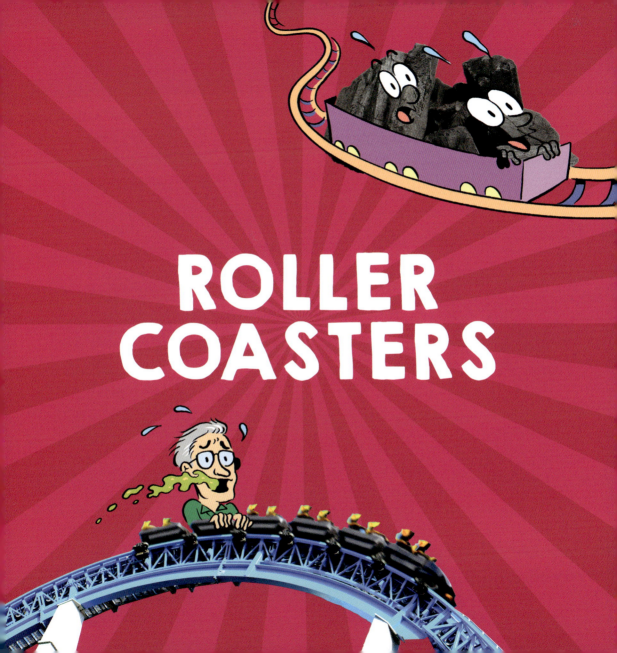

One of the **earliest roller coasters** CARRIED COAL before it carried thrill-seeking humans.

The **TALLEST ROLLER COASTER IN THE WORLD** is the **Kingda Ka** at Six Flags Great Adventure in Jackson, New Jersey.

45 STORIES HIGH!

465-FOOT ASCENT TO THE SKY!

ZERO TO 128 MILES PER HOUR IN ONLY 3.5 SECONDS!

Roller coaster loops are **NEVER** circular.

The **FASTEST ROLLER COASTER** in the world is *Formula Rossa* at Ferrari World in Abu Dhabi. It goes from **ZERO TO 149 MILES PER HOUR** in just **4.9 SECONDS!**

The **LONGEST ROLLER COASTER** is *Steel Dragon 2000* at Nagashima Spa Land in Japan.

It travels 1.5 miles in only four minutes!

Ron Toomer, one of the most famous roller coaster designers, HAD A BAD MOTION SICKNESS PROBLEM.

A **wooden roller coaster** that was built in 1902 is **STILL CARRYING RIDERS TODAY!** The Leap-the-Dips in Altoona, Pennsylvania, goes a whopping **10 MILES PER HOUR** and **DOES NOT HAVE SEATBELTS, LAP BARS, OR HEADRESTS.**

JUST BONKERBALLS

The odds of being BORN AT 12:01 A.M. ON JANUARY 1 are about AS GOOD AS THE ODDS OF BEING STRUCK BY LIGHTNING— that's 1 in 526,000!

Queen Elizabeth II trained as an AUTO MECHANIC.

There are **293 ways** to MAKE CHANGE FOR A U.S. DOLLAR.

On April 18, 1930, an **announcer on the BBC radio network** went on the air and said, "TODAY IS GOOD FRIDAY. THERE IS NO NEWS." Instead, the network played piano music for its audience for the rest of the 15-minute show.

Marie Curie's notebooks are still RADIOACTIVE.

"Positive tickets" are issued by police officers in Canada to people who are **CAUGHT PERFORMING GOOD DEEDS.**

The **unicorn** is the NATIONAL ANIMAL OF SCOTLAND.

The **square dance** is the OFFICIAL DANCE OF 31 STATES.

There is **an island near Mexico City** full of CREEPY, ROTTING BABY DOLLS.

If you **smell something stinky**, it means that the ODOR MOLECULES ARE IN YOUR NOSE!

Atlanta, Illinois, is the ONLY PLACE IN THE WORLD where A GIANT PAUL BUNYON STATUE HOLDS A HOT DOG.

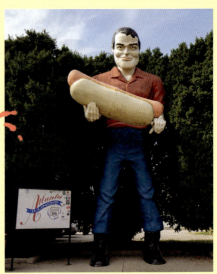

Need ketchup?

In the **Oymyakonsky District** in Russia, the COLDEST INHABITED PLACE on Earth, a human would only be able to survive standing naked outside for ONE MINUTE BEFORE FREEZING TO DEATH.

Every day for nearly one hundred years, a group of **ducks** living in the penthouse of Memphis' Peabody hotel **WADDLE DOWN A RED CARPET TO PLAY IN THEIR FAVORITE LOBBY FOUNTAIN.** It's known as the Peabody Hotel Duck March.

According to the International Sea Glass Museum, **taillights** from underwater cars are the source of the **RAREST COLOR OF SEA GLASS: RED.**

Clarion Books is an imprint of HarperCollins Publishers.

Wow in the World: What in the WOW?! 2
Copyright © 2024 by Tinkercast, LLC
All rights reserved. Manufactured in Malaysia. No part of this book may be used or reproduced in any manner
whatsoever without written permission except in the case of brief quotations embodied in critical articles and
reviews. For information address HarperCollins Children's Books,
a division of HarperCollins Publishers, 195 Broadway, New York, NY 10007.
www.harpercollinschildrens.com

———————————————

Library of Congress Control Number: 2023943262
ISBN 978-0-35-869710-7

———————————————

The illustrations in this book were created digitally using Procreate and Clip Studio Paint.
Typography by Abby Dening
24 25 26 27 28 COS 10 9 8 7 6 5 4 3 2 1

First Edition

 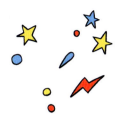

PHOTO CREDITS

24K-Production/Shutterstock: 21 (top right), 28 (top)
3DMAVR/iStockPhoto: 72
5 second Studio/Shutterstock: 36 (top left)
Abdoabdalla/Shutterstock: 134
ADragan/Shutterstock: 65 (bottom)
Aguadeluna/Shutterstock: 33 (top left), 36 (bottom)
AJ_Watt/iStockPhoto: 77 (bottom)
albertogagna/iStockPhoto: 104 (center)
aleks333/Shutterstock: 86 (bottom)
AlexeyVS/iStockPhoto: 61 (top)
aLittleSilhouetto/iStockPhoto: 47 (top)
allanswart/iStockPhoto: 94
Altrendo Images/Shutterstock: 66 (top left)
andresr/iStockPhoto: 38
areallart/Shutterstock: 40 (bottom left)
Artazum/Shutterstock: 132
Noel V. Baebler/Shutterstock: 147
ATTILA Barsan/Shutterstock: 4
barsik/iStockPhoto: 147
bazilfoto/iStockPhoto: 3 (top left), 5 (bottom)
Lance Bellers/Shutterstock: 197 (bottom)
Bespaliy/Shutterstock: 100
Best_photo_studio/Shutterstock: 37 (top), 40 (top), 59 (top left), 60 (bottom)
Bettmann/Getty Images : 23, 109 (top right), 110, 111, 117, 196 (bottom)
Bist/Shutterstock: 129
The Bold Bureau/Shutterstock: 63
buradaki/Shutterstock: 28 (bottom)
Andrey Burmakin/Shutterstock: 86 (top left)
Callipso88/Shutterstock: 200
Cast Of Thousands/Shutterstock: 188 (bottom)
Richie Chan/Shutterstock: 182
Chinch/Shutterstock: 69
Nataliia Chubakova/Shutterstock: 189 (bottom), 193
Julie Clopper/Shutterstock: 37 (bottom left), 43 (top)
Corbis Historical/Getty Images: 131
curtoicurto/iStockPhoto: 178
d_odin/Shutterstock: 157
damedeeso/iStockPhoto: 183
DatHuynh/Shutterstock: 75 (bottom)
Georges De Keerle/Getty Images: 103
Raymond Deleon/Alamy: 67
Different_Brian/iStockPhoto: 140
Dimedrol68/Shutterstock: 66 (bottom center)
doleesi/Shutterstock: 201 (top)
doomu/Shutterstock: 45, 51
Damian DOVARGANES/Getty Images: 54
Dr_Microbe/iStockPhoto: 87
Mike Drosos/Shutterstock: 138
Veronika Dvořáková/iStockPhoto: 73, 82
Elena11/Shutterstock: 26, 30 (top)
enviromantic/iStockPhoto: 90
EpicStockMedia/Shutterstock: 137

erashov/Shutterstock: 167, 174
artault erwan/Getty Images: 30 (bottom)
evenfh/Shutterstock: 158
Everett Collection/Shutterstock: 53 (bottom), 55 (top), 126
f11photo/Shutterstock: 56
Foreverhappy/Shutterstock: 102
Fotosearch/Getty Images: 118
Daniel Fung/Shutterstock: 32 (bottom)
Tatiana Gasich/Shutterstock: 202 (bottom)
Gelpi/Shutterstock: 76
Matt Gibson/Shutterstock: 148–49
Jeff Greenberg/Getty Images: 203 (top)
gremlin/iStockPhoto: 12
Antonio Guillem/Shutterstock: 173 (bottom)
HHelene/iStockPhoto: 14 (bottom)
Hulton Archive/Getty Images: 120 (top)
ilikestudio/Shutterstock: 151
Influcom/Flickr (Creative Commons): 70
iofoto/iStockPhoto: 122
Eric Isselee/Shutterstock: 3 (bottom), 9 (bottom), 10, 17 (bottom), 104 (bottom), 105 (top), 153 (bottom), 154
izusek/iStockPhoto: 172 (bottom)
Jagodka/Shutterstock: 11 (bottom)
Predrag Jankovic/Shutterstock: 83, 96
JBryson/iStockPhoto: 84 (bottom)
JLco - Ana Suanes/iStockPhoto: 77 (top)
Juanmonino/iStockPhoto: 92 (bottom)
Iakov Kalinin/Shutterstock: 184
kamomeen/Shutterstock: 34 (top left)
Palmer Kane LLC/Shutterstock: 201 (bottom)
kapulya/iStockPhoto: 106
Nick Kashenko/Shutterstock: 3 (top right), 9 (top)
katatonia82/Shutterstock: 203 (bottom)
Kazakov/iStockPhoto: 192 (top)
kckate16/Shutterstock: 101 (bottom), 175
ketteimages/Shutterstock: 19 (bottom)
Hans Kim/Shutterstock: 93
Peter Kim/Shutterstock: 199
Serhiy Kobyakov/Shutterstock: 66 (top right)
kornnphoto/Shutterstock: 85 (bottom)
ktaylorg/iStockPhoto: 92 (top)
kudla/Shutterstock: 165
Mark_Kuiken/iStockPhoto: 95
kupicoo/iStockPhoto: 79
lazyllama/Shutterstock: 62 (bottom)
Llgorko/iStockPhoto: 91 (bottom)
likekightctm/Shutterstock: 42 (bottom)
LiliGraphie/Shutterstock: 169
lisegagne/iStockPhoto: 135
livepixx.de/Shutterstock: 152
Lopolo/Shutterstock: 66 (center left)
Lotus_studio/Shutterstock: 34 (top right)
lyash01/iStockPhoto: 156
M Kunz/Shutterstock: 17 (top)

Manook/iStockPhoto: 15
MarkHatfield/iStockPhoto: 39
MartialRed/iStockPhoto: 173 (top)
Thomas Marx/Shutterstock: 20 (top)
Maryia_K/Shutterstock: 42 (top)
MBCheatham/Shutterstock: 91 (top)
Mega Pixel/Shutterstock: 60 (top)
metha1819/Shutterstock: 33 (top right), 36 (top right)
Dean Mitchell/iStockPhoto: 107
Luis Molinero/Shutterstock: 146
monkeybusinessimages/iStockPhoto: 57, 155
M-Production/Shutterstock: 18
mrrabbit2502/iStockPhoto: 88
Nastasic/iStockPhoto: 128
NataSnow/Shutterstock: 7
Andrey Nekrasov/Shutterstock: 16
Vera NewSib/Shutterstock: 46
nimon/Shutterstock: 197 (top)
NVeresk/Shutterstock: 58
Odua Images/Shutterstock: 86 (top right)
Kotomiti Okuma/Shutterstock: 14 (top)
Om.Nom.Nom/Shutterstock: 32 (top), 89
Guillermo Ossa/Shutterstock: 99 (top right), 108 (top)
M. Unal Ozmen/Shutterstock: 59 (bottom), 71
PA Images/Alamy: 19 (top)
Panga Pro/Shutterstock: 163
patrickheagney/iStockPhoto: 75 (top)
PawelG Photo/Shutterstock: 145
Will Pedro/Shutterstock: 48
peepo/iStockPhoto: 24–25
Meeno Peluce: 85 (top)
PeopleImages/iStockPhoto: 196 (top)
Preto Perola/Shutterstock: 143
Vadim.Petrov/Shutterstock: 130
Phonlamai Photo/Shutterstock: 84 (top)
Photobac/Shutterstock: 187 (bottom)
Photoongraphy/Shutterstock: 164
Pictorial Press Ltd/Alamy: 55 (bottom)
Pike-28/Shutterstock: 21 (bottom), 27 (bottom)
pikselstock/Shutterstock: 180 (bottom)
Philip Pilosian/Shutterstock: 59 (top right), 62 (top)
Leah Pirone/Shutterstock: 150, 186
Pit Stock/Shutterstock: 190 (bottom)
piyaphong/Shutterstock: 27 (top)
Alla Pogrebnaya/Shutterstock: 104 (top)
Adrian Popov/Shutterstock: 123
Popperfoto/Getty Images: 29
Andrew Pustiakin/Shutterstock: 185
qingwa/iStockPhoto: 113
Zev Radovan/Alamy: 127
Kunakorn Rassadornyindee/iStockPhoto: 189 (top), 190 (top)
mark reinstein/Shutterstock: 119
Remark_Anna/Shutterstock: 40 (bottom right)
ricochet64/Shutterstock: 64

RnDmS/iStockPhoto: 136
Rocksweeper/Shutterstock: 125 (right)
Eddie J. Rodriquez/Shutterstock: 202 (top)
Roman Samborskyi/Shutterstock: 11 (top)
Romariolen/Shutterstock: 125 (left)
ae san/Shutterstock: 105 (center)
schankz/Shutterstock: 99 (top left), 101 (top)
Science Museum Group Collection: 61 (bottom)
Vaclav Sebek/Shutterstock: 8
dwi septiyana/iStockPhoto: 108 (bottom)
Sergieiev/Shutterstock: 47 (bottom)
Sichon/Shutterstock: 153 (top), 161
Sino Studio/Shutterstock: 160
Carolina K. Smith MD/Shutterstock: 5 (top)
sonap/Shutterstock: 181
Nick Starichenko/Shutterstock: 49
stockphoto mania/Shutterstock: 187 (top)
StockPlanets/iStockPhoto: 168
Stock Up/Shutterstock: 180 (top)
IR Stone/Shutterstock: 74
superbank stock/Shutterstock: 44
Khun Ta/Shutterstock: 52
Denis Tabler/Shutterstock 66 : (middle right)
Diana Taliun/Shutterstock: 37 (bottom right), 41
Vlas Telino studio/Shutterstock: 50
titoOnz/Shutterstock: 65 (top)
Triff/Shutterstock: 31
Suzanne Tucker/Shutterstock: 34 (bottom)
UBC Stock/Shutterstock: 6
Pablo Utrilla/iStockPhoto: 81
Nynke van Holten/iStockPhoto: 105 (bottom)
Dmytro Varavin/iStockPhoto: 78
Various images/Shutterstock: 192 (bottom)
Vejas/Shutterstock: 194
VitaminCo/Shutterstock: 22 (bottom)
vkilikov/Shutterstock: 109 (top left), 112, 120 (bottom)
Aneta Waberska/Shutterstock: 144
Diana Walker/Getty Images: 115
whitemay/iStockPhoto: 116
Ivonne Wierink/Shutterstock: 141, 142
xPACIFICA/Getty Images: 177
gary yim/Shutterstock: 166
Konstantin Yolshin/Shutterstock: 13
Dora Zett/Shutterstock: 188 (top)
Angelina Zinovieva/Shutterstock: 43 (bottom)
ZlataMarka/Shutterstock: 20 (bottom)
alexandre zveiger/Shutterstock: 172 (top)

Don't miss these hilarious books from Wow in the World

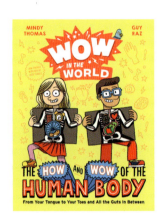
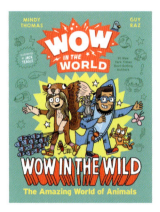

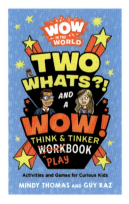